Daily Readings in
Orthodox Spirituality

Titles now available

Daily Readings with Julian of Norwich, vol. 1
Robert Llewelyn
Daily Readings with Julian of Norwich, vol.2
Robert Llewelyn
Daily Readings from The Cloud of Unknowing
Robert Llewelyn
Daily Readings with Brother Lawrence
Robert Llewelyn
Daily Readings with Jean-Pierre de Caussade
Robert Llewelyn
Daily Readings with St Isaac of Syria
A.M. Allchin
Daily Readings with St John of the Cross
Sister Elizabeth Ruth ODC
Daily Readings with St Teresa of Avila
Sister Mary ODC
Daily Readings with St Francis of Assisi
Sister Marie Klepec OSF
Daily Readings with St Francis de Sales
Michael Hollings
Daily Readings from Prayers & Praises in the Celtic Tradition
A.M. Allchin and Esther de Waal
Daily Readings with St Augustine
Dame Maura Sée OSB
Daily Readings with the Desert Fathers
Benedicta Ward SLG

Daily Readings with William Law
Robert Llewelyn and Edward Moss
Daily Readings with St Thérèse of Lisieux
Michael Hollings
Daily Readings with John Wesley
Arthur Skevington Wood
Daily Readings with Martin Luther
James Atkinson
Daily Readings from the Prayers of Samuel Johnson
Elton Trueblood
Daily Readings from Quaker Spirituality
Edward Cell
Daily Readings with Søren Kierkegaard
Robert van de Weyer
Daily Readings with Blaise Pascal
Robert van de Weyer

Daily Readings
in
Orthodox Spirituality

edited by

Peter Bouteneff

TEMPLEGATE PUBLISHERS

Introduction and arrangement © Copyright 1996
Peter Bouteneff

First published in the United States in 1996 by
Templegate Publishers
302 East Adams Street
P.O. Box 5152
Springfield,Illinois 62705

ISBN 0-87243-218-1
Library of Congress Catalog Card Number 95-62274

The fish sign is a symbol used from the very ear-
liest days of Christendom. The letters forming
the word "fish" in Greek, (Ichthys), are the in-
itial letters of five Greek words meaning: "Jesus
Christ, Son of God, Saviour."

Table of contents

Introduction   9

Readings in Orthodox Spirituality   21

Notes, Sources and Biblical References   85

Introduction

The Orthodox Tradition

"I am an Orthodox Christian." In the West, people often find this a confusing statement. Many feel that you have left out the necessary qualifier: "Do you mean Russian Orthodox or Greek Orthodox?" How are we to define this word "Orthodox" in a way that transcends and yet accounts for ethnic backgrounds? What sets apart the Orthodox from other Christians so that we find a book of readings which singles out the "Orthodox" tradition? To begin with, this term has come to be used in two different ways within the Christian context. Historically, and even now, when the lower case "o" is used, it means "right," "proper" or "true," which in Christian usage is (not coincidentally) meant to describe the teachings of the Christian Church, as distinct from doctrines considered as false. Yet particularly since the more decisive split between Christian East and West over the past millennium, "Orthodox" (with the upper case "O") has defined the body of Churches of the Christian East developing through the Byzantine empire on into the present.

"Orthodox" therefore carries both a universal and a particular definition, and of course they overlap. In its broader, or universal sense, it means "true;" and it happens that this particular body of Christians called "Orthodox" believe that what is represented in their tradition is indeed true. But this works the other way around as well: the Orthodox will also say that any word that is true about God, about the created universe, about the human person, is Orthodox, no matter who proclaims it. Ever since St Paul identified the pagans' "unknown God" with God the Father of Jesus Christ,[1] the Church's writers have always accepted certain elements in other belief systems (such as those of the pre-Christian Greeks and Jews) as real truth. The Son of God, the Logos, who became incarnate as Jesus Christ, is universal: He is the one in whom "all things hold together"[2] and because of whom and in whom *logic* or reason exists in the first place. The implication of this universality for a compilation of Orthodox readings is that it might have easily contained certain (though not all) passages from Plato, C.S. Lewis or, for that matter, Tagore alongside the words of St Seraphim of Sarov. Indeed, Fr Gregory Petrov, a twentieth-century Russian priest, was very much in line with the Orthodox Christian tradition when he wrote, shortly before dying in a prison camp, "All true beauty has the power to draw the soul towards Thee and to make it sing in ecstasy: 'Alleluia!'" He continued:

> The breath of Thy Holy Spirit inspires artists, poets, scientists. The power of Thy supreme knowledge makes them prophets and interpreters of Thy laws, who reveal the depths of Thy creative wisdom. Their works speak unwittingly of Thee.[3]

Yet the Orthodox Church, and therefore Orthodox tradition, does represent a particular body, a particular culture. As Church, this body identifies itself with the Church of the apostles, descended to us over the centuries.

Its particularity as a church rests in the sad phenomenon of divisions within the Christian world. These divisions, first of the "Oriental" from the "Eastern" Churches (in the fifth century), and later of the Latin West from the Greek East (commonly dated from the eleventh), have resulted in the fact that one reckons the Roman Catholic Church, and the Protestant Churches which in turn broke from Rome, and the Eastern Orthodox Church as bodies that are distinct one from the other.

Looking at this particularity from a positive angle, however, the Orthodox Church's cultural output represents a specific legacy which emerged out of the predominantly Greek-speaking[4] Byzantine empire, spreading north through Bulgaria, Serbia and Russia. Thus located in the East and the Slavic North, what is now known as the Eastern Orthodox Church developed a spiritual, liturgical, literary and artistic legacy in many ways distinct from that which grew in the West. This geographical location has had broad implications: the art and thought of the Christian East, to give but one major example, was only peripherally affected by the West's Renaissance and its attendant Enlightenment. It developed outside of the action-reaction processes of the Reformation and Counter-Reformation. The evolution of the Eastern Orthodox Church has brought forth a liturgical and iconographic tradition that is particular to itself, as well as a broad literary-spiritual tradition. The purpose of the present book, aside from providing texts for reading and contemplation, is to introduce and celebrate that tradition by selectively dipping into it.

Some readers may wonder about the inclusion of so many ancient writers in this collection and their placement under the banner of "Orthodox Tradition." Are the Church Fathers,[5] especially those from the geographical East, the exclusive property of the Orthodox? Not at all. Yet it can well be argued that the Orthodox have been more thorough in carrying the early Christian writers with them to the present. In their thorough, text-rich liturgical practice which can be observed with a remarkable consistency in almost every Orthodox parish to this day, in the rigorous monastic traditions which also remain thriving, as well as in their typically more conservative theological formulations, the Orthodox as a whole can be said to be more conscious of early patristic and monastic literature than most Western Christians. In any event, the sense of the authority, vitality and eternal relevance of the Church's patristic and liturgical texts and rites—indeed, the sense that these form the proper context for the understanding of Scripture itself—helps to explain their preponderance in the present compilation.

While the Orthodox Church does have a powerful sense of its early patristic roots, it would be quite wrong to say that its spring has dried up in the modern world, or that it has remained in the geographical East. It is basic to the teaching of the Orthodox that Tradition (which in turn is associated, if not identified, with the activity of the Holy Spirit) is something that is always kinetic, alive, breathing everywhere and at every moment. The Christian truth is constantly finding new expression and new formulations, whose genuineness is gauged by their fidelity to that tradition which produced the Bible as well as other *loci theologici*[6] through history, be they written on pages, sung in church, painted on boards or walls, or lived as holy lives. Thus, while there are times and places of patristic flourishing, such as fourth-century Asia Minor or fourteenth-century Russia, Orthodox Fathers, saints, writings, icons, liturgical texts are capable of being produced in any age, in any place.

With the increased movement of people and cultures after the Middle Ages and the subsequent expansion of the Orthodox Church to the whole world, this universal potential for producing holy texts (some of which might even be called "neo-patristic"), holy icons, holy lives (saints), springing from the same font of living tradition, has borne much fruit. This range of expression, through time and place, from early Hellenic and Semitic Byzantium, through the Balkans and Russia, and contemporary Europe and America is something that I have tried to reflect in the readings selected here.

Insofar as they are representative of the Orthodox tradition, these readings will inevitably highlight certain emphases within the Orthodox tradition, which might benefit from being introduced, however briefly:[7]

Asceticism

If the word "Orthodox" is a source of confusion for many a modern reader, this is much more the case for the concept of asceticism. Asceticism is a term usually thought to denote an especially austere lifestyle, prescribed for a particularly rigorous or perhaps even masochistic few. Indeed, it is usually considered in terms of renunciation, or what one *doesn't* do. But the Eastern Church writers would by-and-large rather have us understand asceticism in positive terms (23,29,33). Asceticism is seen as synonymous with "a Christian mode of life," oriented towards everything that life can and should be. Olivier Clément expressed well the positive nature of Christian asceticism:

> Asceticism is not obedience to some abstract categorical imperative. It frees human nature to follow its deep instinct to ascend towards God. It enables a person to pass from a state "contrary to nature" to a state "in harmony with nature," in harmony, that is, with that human (and cosmic) material united in Christ with the godhead, without separation or confusion. [8]

Asceticism therefore points us in the right direction. This is the way it must be understood, not as something that invites gloom. It is said of St Seraphim, the great ascetic and abbot of Sarov (48), that although he did not allow evil talk or anything malicious, he never forbade anyone from being merry. Even when the Church invites us to take a hard, penitential look at ourselves, such as in the Great Canon of St Andrew of Crete (58,59), the context of self condemnation is an awareness of the goodness of creation, the goodness which we are constantly failing to live up to, and particularly the supra-goodness of the Creator. Repentance, which means "change of mind," is a redirection upwards, brought about by the always simultaneous realization of one's own failings on the one hand, and the unending glory of God on the other. With this realization comes an awed understanding of the total and loving forgiveness of God (24,25).

Asceticism, thus defined, is intended for everyone. True, certain ascetical writings are specifically directed towards monastic readership, but most are explicitly universal. This is the case even for the *Philokalia,* that broad and beloved compilation of ascetical literature so central to Orthodox spirituality. In his introduction to this anthology, St Nicodemos of the Holy Mountain invites everyone to

> come and eat the bread of knowledge and wisdom, and drink the wine which spiritually delights the heart...and becomes inebriated with the truly alert inebriation. Come all...together, lay people and monastics, all of you who seek to find the kingdom of God which is within you, as well as the treasure which is hidden in the field of your heart. And this is the sweet Christ.[9]

Yet even those writings that are intended for monastics have in them much to be gleaned by the rest of us. Metropolitan Anthony Bloom, head of the Russian Orthodox Church in England, wrote about the desert fathers, whose extremism can at times appear to be almost freakish: "These were men and women who had reached a humility of which we have no idea, because it is not rooted in a hypocritical or contrived depreciation of self, but in the vision of God, and a humbling experience of being so loved."[10] We must therefore be mindful of context — who is writing, who is the intended reader, how does this fit in with the larger picture? Only then can we take writers such as the desert ascetics on their own terms and figure out what it all means for us.

Of course, this necessity for an awareness of context poses a virtually unsolvable problem for a book of daily readings which, limited as it were to a few sound-bites of spirituality, can only take one so far. The notes accompanying each selection are meant to be a slight help; the interested reader might wish to pursue further study.

Prayer

The present book contains several passages on prayer, as well as the texts of several prayers. The prayers' character and the concerns that they express might be thought of as classically Orthodox — note especially the human qualities we pray for, exemplified in St Ephrem's lenten prayer (53), the desire in our prayers to be attuned to God's will and to fulfill it (46,82), the practical concern for every person and his or her need (34), as well as for the created earth itself, its fruitfulness, its good estate — this created world which is continually proclaimed as something *good*.

Orthodox spirituality in general, and the Orthodox practice of prayer in particular, is often associated with "mysticism" — yet another potentially confusing term. The association of Orthodoxy with mysticism is quite apt, provided one defines mysticism as pertaining to our journey towards union with God, and not as something involving secret teachings, a lofty idea available to a select few, or something achieved as an end in itself by way of a technique. As Vladimir Lossky affirms in his classic *The Mystical Theology of the Eastern Church,*[11] all theology is mystical, and should have an eminently practical significance. Prayer might be essentially defined as a state of being (54,55), and yet it is focused in our specific words addressed to God. Let us take the example of the Jesus prayer — "Lord Jesus Christ, Son of God, have mercy upon me." While this prayer, especially when said repetitively, can rightly be called a "way," a state, a vocation, before it is anything else it is a cry from one person to another, which is part of a relationship between the human person and Jesus Christ, the Son of the living God. Without this primary, practical, *personal* foundation, Christian "mysticism" is standing on no ground at all.

Of the prayers featured in this book, some are written for corporate, liturgical use, and some for private use. It must be noted that personal prayer and the corporate prayer of the Church's liturgy are strongly interrelated (35). The Fathers took it as a given that private prayer, particularly the Jesus prayer and "the way of stillness" (or hesychasm), has its living roots in the communal prayer of the Church — the wide-ranging prayers of the liturgy in its daily, weekly, yearly cycles of fasting and feasting, all crowned by the Church's sacramental life (41). As noted above, this is the context for the understanding of scripture, and, by extension, of reality. It also provides the nourishment and guidance of each person's prayer life. And finally, as Tito Colliander (21) writes, "prayer is action, to pray is to be highly effective." Prayer, whether in a church or a monastic cell, is a social action, uniting us in communion with each other as well as with the Divine. Yet, as St John Chrysostom (38), and Mother Maria of Paris (39) remind us, prayer does not absolve us of the responsibility of actually feeding the hungry, visiting the sick, housing the homeless — it calls us to that activity and serves as its context.

Human Freedom

Within this patristic emphasis upon asceticism and prayer there is the sense, sometimes explicit and sometimes implied, of the goodness of creation, particularly the goodness of the human person. Man's creation in the image of God is a powerful current in Orthodox teaching, and a part of that divine image consists in man's *freedom*. That innate freedom, which cannot be taken away despite the great efforts of despotic governments and societies driven by consumerism, is a great gift and yet a great cross for us. Human freedom has meant, for the Orthodox, that ethical or moral decisions are based less upon a set of established codes and more upon the vision of what human life is meant to be: freely chosen, loving communion with God here and now. Human freedom dictates that morality, and even salvation itself, is not to be viewed in juridical terms. Great significance is placed upon our reception and response to what is given us in our own particular situation.

Of course, this responsibility is one that we would often rather not have. So often, we would rather have our religion brought to us on a platter, our behavior dictated to us through a series of rules we must follow to arrive at a clearly-defined happy end. Or perhaps we would prefer to have been created as automatically moral beings who would consistently choose to be in harmony and union with the loving God. Instead we are presented with a single standard, which is nothing other than a sense of the glory of life, and the awesome glory and love of the Life-giver. How stunning that we fallen people tend away from this glory! In this choice lies the basis for all the suffering in the world. The joy and pain of human freedom, human suffering and its sublimation through Christ into a means of growth towards God — these themes run deep in Orthodox spirituality, from patristic writings to the essays of Berdyaev and the novels of Dostoevsky.

*

The spirituality of the Orthodox Church is broad, coming as it does from a huge variety of places, persons and concerns. If nothing else, it knows and travels the extremes of reality: the depth of the human fall (58) and the height of the super-abundant glory and goodness of God. The Orthodox Church is a divine-human entity, and in its fallen human capacity it so often has failed to live up to its calling to be the ever-living witness of God in creation and the offerer of creation to God. In its justifiable love for the early Church fathers and for ancient practices, it has often resisted change and creativity. In its natural and vital ties with particular places, nations and ethnicities, it has often come to exalt national identity over

Christianity. Yet it is so very rich in what it offers, so full of surprises. Fr Lev Gillet (1893-1980) expressed this paradox eloquently:

> O strange Orthodox Church, so poor and so weak, at the same time so traditional and yet so free, so archaic and yet so alive, so ritualistic and yet so personally mystical, Church where the pearl of great price of the Gospel is preciously preserved, sometimes beneath a layer of dust — Church that has so often proved incapable of action, yet which knows, as does no other, how to sing the joy of Easter.[12]

* * *

Those wishing to delve further into the sources are directed to the two classic introductions by Kallistos Ware: *The Orthodox Church,* which focuses on the Church's history and composition, and *The Orthodox Way,* which is more concerned with its inner life. Both books have recently been revised and feature extensive bibliographies. Also highly recommended is Oliver Clément's collection entitled *The Roots of Christian Mysticism.*[13]

It is hoped that the readings in this book will provide a glimpse into the joyous breadth of the Orthodox tradition. I am indebted to many friends for their suggestions.

Peter Bouteneff

Starting Here and Now

If you wish to save your soul and win eternal life, arise from your lethargy, make the sign of the Cross and say: In the name of the Father, and of the Son and of the Holy Spirit. Amen.

Faith comes not through pondering but through action. Not words and speculation but experience teaches us what God is. To let in fresh air we have to open a window; to get tanned we must go out into the sunshine. Achieving faith is no different; we never reach a goal by just sitting in comfort and waiting, say the holy Fathers. Let the Prodigal Son be our example. He *arose and came.*[14]

However weighed down and entangled in earthly fetters you might be, it can never be too late. Not without reason is it written that Abraham was seventy-five when he set forth, and the laborer who comes in the eleventh hour gets the same wages as the one who comes in the first.

No, this moment, the instant you make your resolution, you will show by your action that you have taken leave of your old self and have now begun a new life, and with a new destination and a new way of living. Arise, therefore, without fear and say: Lord, let me begin now. Help me! For what we need above all is God's help.

Tito Colliander

Come in Freedom

He who is sinless, but not of his own free will, is not praiseworthy. Otherwise we would praise those people who are in chains, prevented by their chains from doing evil. It is their chains, not their will, that keep them from evil.

*

[Therefore, when you ascend to perfection,] come, says the Word, by yourself; not out of sadness or a sense of compulsion, but by yourself, confirming your desire for the good by your own reason, and not out of any necessity. For perfection must not be coerced, it must be voluntary and free of all constraint. Such was David, for he realized that of all the things that he had done, only those were pleasing to God that were done freely, and so he vows that he will freely offer sacrifice. And this is the spirit of every saint of God, not to be led by necessity.

St Gregory of Nyssa

Come in Love

God, who "wishes all to be saved and to come to the knowledge of the truth,"[15] shows the most perfect and blessed way of salvation — I mean the way of love.

For some there is salvation by fear: we contemplate the threat of punishment in hell and so avoid evil. But the person who is hastening to spiritual perfection rejects fear. Such a disposition is servile, and the person with this disposition does not remain with the master out of love. He stays put out of fear of being scourged.

Then, there are those who conduct themselves virtuously out of the hope of a reward for a life piously lived. They do not possess the good out of love but out of the expectation of recompense.

But the person seeking perfection disdains even rewards: he does not prefer the gift to the one who bestows it. He loves, "with his whole heart and soul and strength,"[16] him who is the source of all good things. This, then, is the attitude which he commands to the souls of all who listen to him, for he summons us to share his own life.

St Gregory of Nyssa

God's Written Assurance

It often happens that Satan will insidiously commune with you in your heart and say: "Think of the evil you have done; your soul is full of lawlessness, you are weighed down by many grievous sins." Do not let him deceive you when he does this and do not be led to despair on the pretext that you are being humble. After gaining admission through the fall, evil has the power to commune at all times with the soul, as man to man, and so to suggest sinful actions to it. You should answer it: "I have God's written assurance, for He says, 'I desire not the death of the sinner, but that he should return through repentance and live' " (cf. Ezek. 33:11). What was the purpose of His descent to earth except to save sinners, to bring light to those in darkness and life to the dead?

Macarian Homilies

Sin and Forgiveness

Let us arrive at a knowledge of the dignity of our nature, and also a clear perception of the loving-kindness of God. Indeed, this will prevent us from even looking at anything evil, and should we happen to fall it will readily raise us up again.

Of the many things which impede our salvation the greatest of all is that when we commit any transgression we do not at once turn back to God and ask forgiveness. Because we feel shame and fear we think that the way back to God is difficult, and that He is angry and ill-tempered towards us, and that there is need of great preparation if we wish to approach Him. But the loving-kindness of God utterly banishes this thought from the soul. What can prevent anyone who clearly knows how kind He is and that, as it is said, "while you are yet speaking He will say, 'Here I am,'"[17] from approaching Him at once for pardon of the sins which he has committed?

St Nicholas Cabasilas

The Signs of Stillness

The following are the signs, the stages, and the proofs of practicing stillness in the right way: a calm mind, a purified disposition, rapture in the Lord, the remembrance of everlasting torments, the imminence of death, an insatiable urge for prayer, constant watchfulness, the death of lust, no sense of attachment, death of worldliness, an end to gluttony, a foundation for divine contemplation, a well of discernment, a truce accompanied by tears, an end to talkativeness, and many other such things alien to most people.

The following are signs of stillness practiced wrongly — poverty of spiritual treasures, anger on the increase, a growth of resentment, love diminished, a surge of vanity. And I will say nothing about all that follows from these.

St John Climacus

God is the Life of All

God is the life of all free beings. He is the salvation of all, of believers and unbelievers, of the just and the unjust, of the pious or the impious, of those freed from the passions or caught up in them, of monks and those living in the world, of the educated or the illiterate, of the healthy or the sick, of the young or the very old. He is like the outpouring of light, the glimpse of the sun, or the changes of the weather, which are the same for everyone without exception.

St John Climacus

Run Without Ceasing, and Rejoice

Run without ceasing the road which has been prepared, so that you may reach with joy the haven of Christ, and hear the voice which is full of joy and life and rejoicing, say to you, "Well done, good and faithful servant. You have been faithful over a little, I will set you over much. Enter into the joy of your Lord."[18] Rejoice in the Lord! Rejoice in the Lord! Rejoice in the Lord! May the Lord protect your soul and your body and your spirit from every evil...and from every diabolical opposition and from every disturbing fantasy. The Lord will be your light, your protection, your way, your strength, a crown of rejoicing and eternal help.

St Barsanuphius the Great

Glory in this Life

Who can imagine, who can search out the indescribable joy, the inexpressible gladness, the unimaginable light which the saints experience? While they are yet in this life God reveals to them his wonderful, glorious mysteries, the glory and refreshment that await them. He alters their minds, detaching them from this world, so that they may always see themselves in heaven with Christ and the angels. Neither hunger nor thirst nor any other earthly thing afflicts them, for they have been set free from all the accusations, passions and sins of this life.

*

May the God of our Fathers bring you to this joy, for it is unutterable light; it is resplendent; it is sweet. It does not remember physical food, for it has forgotten to eat its bread.[19] It has its mind elsewhere: it seeks the things above, thinks on the things above, meditates on the things above, where Christ sits on the right hand of the Father. To Him be the glory to the ages, Amen.

St Barsanuphius the Great

Children of God

Those who have been deemed worthy to become children of God and to be reborn by the Holy Spirit, who have within themselves Christ, illuminating and bringing them rest, are guided in many and various ways by the Spirit....Sometimes they find themselves immersed in weeping and lamenting over the whole human race; they pray for the "whole Adam" with tears, inflamed as they are with spiritual love for all humanity. At times also their spirit is kindled with such joy and such love that, if it were possible, they would gather every human being into their very hearts, without distinguishing the bad and good. Sometimes again in the humility received from the Spirit, they humble themselves before every human being, so they consider themselves to be the last and least important of all beings. After which the Spirit makes them live afresh in ineffable joy.

Macarian Homilies

The Compassionate Heart

An elder was once asked, "What is a compassionate heart?" He replied:

"It is a heart on fire for the whole of creation, for humanity, for the birds, for the animals, for demons and for all that exists. At the recollection and at the sight of them such a person's eyes overflow with tears owing to the vehemence of the compassion which grips his heart; as a result of his deep mercy his heart shrinks and cannot bear to hear or look upon any injury or the slightest suffering of anything in creation. This is why he constantly offers up prayer full of tears, even for the irrational animals and for the enemies of truth, even for those who harm him, so that they may be protected and find mercy. He even prays for the reptiles as a result of the great compassion which is poured out beyond measure — after the likeness of God — in his heart."

St Isaac the Syrian

The Miracle of Condescension

It belongs to the nature of fire to shoot upwards, and no one would think it wonderful for a flame to act naturally. But if he saw a flame with a downward motion like that of heavenly bodies, he would take it for a marvel, wondering how it could remain a flame and yet contravene its nature by its downward motion. So it is with the incarnation. God's transcendent power is not so much displayed in the vastness of the heavens, or the luster of the stars, or the orderly arrangement of the universe or his perpetual oversight of it, as in his condescension to our weak nature. We marvel at the way the sublime entered a state of lowliness and, while actually seen in it, did not leave the heights. We marvel at the way the Godhead was entwined in human nature and, while becoming man, did not cease to be God.

St Gregory of Nyssa

The Human Person and the God-Man

[We are not talking about] some abstract, super-heavenly God of Plato or Kant, but about a God of concrete earthly reality, a God who became man and infuses into human categories all that is divine, immortal and eternal. Therefore, only this one among the human race, namely, the God-man Christ, had the right to seek from men divine perfection ("You therefore, must be perfect, as your heavenly Father is perfect")[20] and to place divine perfection as the goal of life and as the goal of the whole endeavor of man. By doing this, He gives to humans at the same time all the necessary means and all the necessary strength with which to realize this goal of obtaining divine perfection.

What are these means? The holy gospel-oriented virtues: faith and love, fasting and prayer, meekness and humility, compassion and goodness, hope and patience, truth and justice. Applying these virtues produces a holy person, namely, a perfect and complete person. Such a person knows the real meaning of the world and of life, and he lives with his whole being directed towards realizing his given purpose in the arena of human activity.

Justin Popovich

Remember, O Lord, All Thy People

Fill their treasuries with every good thing; preserve their marriages in peace and harmony, raise the infants, guide the young, support the aged, encourage the fainthearted, reunite the separated, lead back those who are in error and join them to Thy Holy, Catholic and Apostolic Church; free those who are held captive by unclean spirits, sail with those who sail, travel with those who travel by land and by air, defend the widows, protect the orphans, free the captives, heal the sick. Remember, O God, those who are in courts, in mines, in exile, in harsh labor, and those in any kind of affliction, necessity or distress. Remember, O Lord our God, ...those who love us and those who hate us...and remember all Thy people, O Lord our God. ...Visit us with Thy loving-kindness, O Lord; manifest Thyself to us through Thy rich compassions. Grant us seasonable and healthful weather; send gentle showers upon the earth so that it may bear fruit; bless the crown of the year with Thy goodness...Receive us all into Thy Kingdom, showing us to be children of the light and children of the day. Grant us Thy peace and Thy love, O Lord our God, for Thou hast given all things to us.

Liturgy of St Basil the Great

Increasing the talent of Grace

Come, ye faithful, and let us serve the Master eagerly,
for He gives riches to His servants.
Each of us according to the measure we have received,
let us increase the talent of grace.
Let one gain wisdom through good deeds;
let another celebrate the Liturgy with splendor;
let another communicate the word to those untaught;
let another give his wealth to the poor.
So shall we increase what is entrusted to us,
and as faithful stewards of His grace
we shall be counted worthy of the Master's joy.
Bestow this joy upon us, Christ our God,
in Thy love for mankind.

Sung during Holy Week

Prayer in Church

Both public and private prayer are necessary in order that we may lead a truly Christ-like life, and that the life of the spirit should not become extinct in us. It is indispensable that we should attend divine service in church with faith, zeal and understanding, just as it is indispensable to provide a lamp with fuel or power if it is to burn and not go out.

During divine service be trustful, as a child trusts his parents. Be simple, trustful, undoubting, as a child, in godly matters. Cast all your care upon the Lord, and be entirely free from sorrow: *Take no thought how or what ye shall speak: for it shall be given you in that same hour when you shall speak. For it is not ye that speak, but the Spirit of your Father, which speaketh in you.*[21] Long ago the Lord freed us from this care, having by His Spirit taught the Church what to say, how to pray at divine service.

St John of Kronstadt

Flowers for God

People who believe in God in their own way, yet do not believe in the Church, often say, "Does God really need all this ritual? Why do we have to have all these formalities? We only need love, beauty and humaneness." A man, on his way to the woman he loves, seeing flowers, buys them or picks them and brings them to her, never stopping to think whether this is a formality or not. Yet this is the very concept of church ritual.

Love for God gives birth to the beauty and humanity of the ritual, which we lay, like flowers, at the feet of God. Faith is love, and the essence of Christianity is to be in love with God and to feel that the Church is His body which has remained with us and lives with us on earth. This feeling expresses itself in actions which we call ritual.

However, if only external and dead action remains, then such action will be sterile and self-deceptive, not only in Christianity but in any sphere of human life, even in science. This truth should be clear to everyone.

Formalism and sanctimoniousness is not Christianity. Each one of us has to move along this long and narrow way from non-Christianity to Christianity, from artificial flowers to live ones.

Fr Sergei Fudel

Eucharist and Responsibility

Ponder the nature of the Eucharistic offering itself. Christ is there, sacrificed. And for what purpose was he sacrificed? To bring peace to the things of heaven and earth, to reconcile you with the God of the universe and make you his friend...What the Son of God has done in this way, you must do too as your human strength allows, by being a builder of peace both for yourself and for others....That is why at the moment of the sacrifice, the only commandment of which he reminds you is to be reconciled with your brother. Thus he shows you that this is more important than the others.

*

Do you wish to honor the body of the Savior? Do not despise it when it is naked. Do not honor it in church with silk vestments while outside you are leaving it naked and numb with cold. He who said, "This is my body," and made it so by his word, is the same that said, "You saw me hungry and you gave me no food. As you did it not to the least of these, you did it not to me." Honor him then by sharing your property with the poor. For what God needs is not golden chalices but golden souls.

St John Chrysostom

The Way to God

The way to God lies through love of people, and there is no other way. At the Last Judgment I shall not be asked whether I was successful in my ascetic exercises, how many bows and prostrations I made [in the course of prayer]. I shall be asked, Did I feed the hungry, clothe the naked, visit the sick and the prisoners. That is all I shall be asked. About every poor, hungry and imprisoned person the Savior says "I": "I was hungry and thirsty, I was sick and in prison." [22] To think that he puts an equal sign between himself and anyone in need...I always knew it, but now it has somehow penetrated into my sinews. It fills me with awe.

Mother Maria Skobtsova

Reproving Excess

Do not devote yourself entirely to disciplining your body. Arrange a program that is within your capability and then concentrate on what is within. "Bodily asceticism has only a limited use, but true devotion is useful in all things." [23]

He who always concentrates on the inner life becomes restrained, patient, kind and humble. He will also be able to contemplate, theologize and pray. This is what St Paul meant when he said, "Walk in the Spirit." [24]

One ignorant of this spiritual path is not on his guard against impassioned conceptual images, but lets himself be entirely taken up with the body. He either becomes gluttonous, licentious, full of resentment, anger and rancor, darkening his intellect as a result, or he overdoes asceticism and loses his clarity of thought.

Not one of the things God has put at our disposal is forbidden in Scripture. The Bible limits itself to reproving excess and correcting what is unreasonable. For example, it does not forbid us from eating, having children, possessing wealth and administering it properly, only avoid gluttony, fornication, and so on. It does not forbid us to think of these things — they were made to be thought of — avoid only dwelling on them with immoderate eagerness.

St Maximus the Confessor

Communion: The Daily Bread

Holy Communion illumines, brightens, and sanctifies all the powers and senses of man's soul and body, and strengthens the soul in doing the commandments of the Lord and every other virtuous act. It is the true food of the soul and of the body, as our Lord says, "My flesh is food indeed, and my blood is drink indeed."[25]

Common bread is improperly called our daily bread, because it strengthens only our body and not our soul. Properly and principally the term "daily bread" denotes the body of our Lord and the word of God, because they strengthen the soul as well as the body. For this reason, those of us who have received spiritual regeneration through divine Baptism must continually eat this spiritual food with warm love and a contrite heart.

Just as breathing is necessary for life, and just as food is necessary for the sustenance of the body, so is frequent Communion necessary for the life of the soul and for the sustenance of its substance, or rather it is incomparably more necessary.

St Macarius of Corinth

The Struggle and the Kingdom

Amma Theodora said, "Let us strive to enter by the narrow gate. Just as the trees, if they have not stood before the winter's storms cannot bear fruit, so it is with us; this present age is a storm and it is only through many trials and temptations that we can obtain an inheritance in the kingdom of heaven."

Amma Syncletica said, "Great endeavors and hard struggles await those who are converted, but afterwards inexpressible joy. If you want to light a fire, you are troubled at first by smoke, and your eyes water. But in the end you achieve your aim. Now it is written: 'Our God is a consuming fire.' So we must light the divine fire in us with tears and struggle."

Temptation and Humility

Abba Anthony said to Abba Poemen, "This is the great work of a man: always to take the blame for his own sins before God and to expect temptation to his last breath."

He also said, "Whoever has not experienced temptation cannot enter into the Kingdom of Heaven." He even added, "Without temptations, no one can be saved."

He also said, "I saw all the snares that the enemy spreads out over the world and I said groaning, 'What can get one through such snares?' Then I heard a voice saying to me, 'Humility.'"

Hearing the Lord's Voice

"Behold, I stand at the door and knock; if anyone hears my voice and opens the door, I will come in to him and eat with him and he with me".[26]

...How often have we stood weeping looking far away up to heaven where we think the Lord Jesus lives! He is present and standing before us, and all that prevents us from encountering Him is our heart's lack of perception! How often have we stood praying before Him, begging Him to speak to us, hoping that we might hear Him, but it was useless! He never stops calling us by name; nothing prevents us from hearing His voice but our preoccupation with our own daily problems.

The mistake we make is that we want to see Him in the midst of the daily events that fill our mental and emotional emptiness. But in fact the Lord is present now beyond all these things, beyond time and events, which He controls according to His own wise plan. The alert and simple soul notices the touch of His hand writing the story of its salvation through the years and succession of events. Our successes and failures work together in a positive way guided by the Almighty for our salvation. Temporal losses are not spiritual losses, and trouble, sadness, pain and sickness are the language of divine providence, its secret code, which when deciphered in the Spirit spells resurrection, joy, and eternal glory.

Matta El-Meskin (Matthew the Poor)

God's Inscrutable Will

Two brothers were going to see Anthony. On their journey they ran out of water and one of the two died. The other was at death's door. At the end of his strength he lay down on the ground awaiting death. Anthony, sitting on the mountain side, called two monks who were there and urged them, "Take a jug of water and hurry to the road from Egypt. Two brothers were coming. One of them is already dead, and the other is going to die unless you are quick. This has just been revealed to me in prayer." The monks went and found the dead monk and buried him. Then they refreshed the exhausted one with a drink of water and took him to the elder. The distance was a day's journey. Someone perhaps will ask, "Why did not Anthony speak before the first monk died?" That would be wrong. It was no business of Anthony's to determine the time of his death. That is reserved to God, and God decreed death for the one and revealed to Anthony the danger in which the other was.

St Athanasius of Alexandria's Life of Anthony

Doing the Will of God

The best thing of all is to surrender to God's will, and bear affliction with confidence in God. The Lord seeing our affliction will never give us too much to bear. If we seem to ourselves to be greatly afflicted, it means that we have not surrendered to the will of God.

The soul that is in all things devoted to the will of God rests tranquil in Him, for she knows of experience and from the Holy Scriptures that the Lord loves us much and watches over our souls, quickening all things by His grace and love.

Nothing troubles the man who is given over to the will of God, be it illness, poverty, persecution. He knows that the Lord in His mercy is solicitous for us. The Holy Spirit, Whom the soul knows, is witness thereof. But the proud and the self-willed do not want to surrender to God's will because they like their own way, and that is harmful for the soul.

St Silouan the Athonite

Inspiration

Truly holy inspiration, proceeding from the Father on High, does not impose itself. It must be obtained, like every other gift from God, by an urgent effort of prayer. This does not signify that God gives some sort of "reward" for effort made but that what one has acquired through cognizant suffering becomes an inalienable possession for eternity. It is imperative for every one of us to be totally reborn by the action of grace; that the ability to apprehend divinization be restored in us. But all this is possible in no other way than by our return to Him — a return involving much torment.

...Inspiration from on High depends to a considerable extent on us, on whether we open our heart so that the Lord — the Holy Spirit who "stands at the door and knocks" — does not have to enter forcibly. If anyone hears His voice and opens the door, He will come to him, and will sup with him, and he with God.[27] The Lord preserves the freedom of those created "in His image." And we have to know what is acceptable to Him. Hence the need for each and all of us to ban deeds and impulses which may grieve the Spirit of God. Honest abiding in the sphere of Christ's commandments heals our sinful mortality, and all life becomes penetrated by the Uncreated Light of Divine Eternity.

Archimandrite Sophrony

Acquiring the Holy Spirit

Prayer, fasting, watching may be good in themselves, yet it is not in these practices alone that the goal of our Christian life is to be found, though they are the necessary means for its attainment. The true goal consists in our acquiring the Holy Spirit of God. Fasting and watching, alms and all good works done for the sake of Christ are the means of acquiring the Holy Spirit of God. Great is the power of prayer; more than anything else it brings the Spirit of God. Through prayer we receive the privilege of conversing with God our Savior himself, all-bountiful and life-giving.

St Seraphim of Sarov

Come, Holy Spirit

O Heavenly King,
The Comforter, the Spirit of Truth
Who art everywhere and fillest all things
Treasury of good things, and giver of life
Come and abide in us,
And cleanse us from every impurity
And save our souls, O Good One!

*

Every soul is enlivened by the Holy Spirit,
And is exalted in purity,
Illumined by the Holy Trinity
In a sacred mystery.

Prayer is God

In the relationship of prayer, it is the divine partner and not the human who takes the initiative and whose action is fundamental. In his effort to describe the true reality of inner prayer, [Gregory of Sinai] ends suddenly with unexpected simplicity: "Why speak at length? Prayer is God, who works all things in all men." *Prayer is God* — not something that I initiate but something in which I share; it is not primarily something that *I* do but something that *God* is doing in me: St Paul's phrase, "Not I, but Christ in me." [28] The path of inner prayer is exactly indicated in St John the Baptist's words about the Messiah: "He must increase, but I must decrease." [29] It is in this sense that to pray is to be silent. "You yourself must be silent; let the prayer speak" — more precisely, let God speak.

Bishop Kallistos of Diokleia

That God Pray in Us

O Lord, grant me to greet the coming day in peace. In every hour of the day reveal Thy will to me. Bless my dealing with all who surround me. Teach me to treat all that comes to me throughout the day with peace of soul, and with firm conviction that Thy will governs all. In all my deeds and words guide my thoughts and feelings. In unforeseen events let me not forget that all are sent by Thee. Teach me to act firmly and wisely, without embittering or embarrassing others. Give me strength to bear the fatigue of the coming day with all that it shall bring. Direct my will, teach me to pray, pray Thou Thyself in me. Amen.

*

O Lord, I know not what to ask of Thee. Thou alone knowest what are my true needs. Thou lovest me more than I myself know how to love. Help me to see my real needs which are concealed from me. I dare not ask either a cross or a consolation. I can only wait on Thee. My heart is open to Thee. Visit and help me, for Thy great mercy's sake. Strike me and heal me, cast me down and raise me up. I worship in silence Thy holy will and Thine inscrutable ways. I offer myself as a sacrifice to Thee. I put all my trust in Thee. I have no other desire than to fulfill Thy will. Teach me how to pray. Pray Thou Thyself in me. Amen.

Philaret of Moscow

A Prayer for All Hours

Thou who, at all times and at every hour, both in heaven and on earth, art worshipped and glorified, O Christ-God, long-suffering and plenteous in mercy and compassion; who lovest the just and showest mercy to those who are hardened in sin; who callest all to salvation through the promise of good things to come: Do Thou, the same Lord, receive also our supplications at this present time, and direct our lives according to Thy commandments. Sanctify our souls, purify our bodies, set aright our minds, cleanse our thoughts, and deliver us from all calamity, anger and distress. Compass us round about with Thy holy Angels; that, guided and guarded by their host, we may attain to the unity of faith, and unto the comprehension of Thine ineffable glory. For blessed art Thou unto ages of ages. Amen.

Prayer of the Hours

A Lenten Prayer

O Lord and Master of my life,
give me not a spirit of sloth,
despair, lust for power,
and idle talk.

But give rather a spirit of sobriety,
humility, patience and love
to me, Thy servant.

Yea, O Lord and King
grant me to see my own errors
and not to judge my brother,

For blessed art Thou unto ages of ages,
Amen.

Lenten prayer of St Ephrem the Syrian

One Center, One Point

"Lord Jesus Christ, Son of God, Have Mercy on Me"

The Jesus Prayer is a prayer in words, but because the words are so simple, so few and unvarying, the Prayer reaches out beyond words into the living silence of the Eternal. It is a way of achieving, with God's assistance, the kind of non-discursive, non-iconic prayer in which we do not simply make statements to or about God, in which we do not just form pictures of Christ in our imagination, but are 'oned' with him in an all-embracing, unmediated encounter. Through the Invocation of the Name we feel his nearness with our spiritual sense, much as we feel the warmth with our bodily senses on entering a heated room. We know him, not through a series of successive images and concepts, but with the unified sensibility of the heart. So the Jesus Prayer concentrates us into the *here* and *now*, making us single-centered, one-pointed, drawing us from a multiplicity of thoughts to union with the one Christ. "Through the remembrance of Jesus Christ," says St Philotheus of Sinai, "gather together your scattered intellect" — gather it together from the plurality of discursive thinking into the simplicity of love.

Bishop Kallistos of Diokleia

Homo Adorans

In the catacombs, the most frequent image is the figure of a woman in prayer, the *Orant*; she represents the one true attitude of the human soul. It is not enough to *say* prayers; one must become, *be* prayer, prayer incarnate. It is not enough to have moments of praise. All of life, each act, every gesture, even the smile of the human face, must become a hymn of adoration, an offering, a prayer. One should offer not what one has, but what one is....It translates the message of the Gospel: *khaíre*, "rejoice and be glad," "let everything that has breath praise the Lord." This is the astonishing lightening of the weight of the world, when man's own heaviness vanishes.

Paul Evdokimov

Worthy to Do Thy Will

O Lord our God, remember us Thy sinful and unprofitable servants when we call upon Thy holy and venerable name, and put us not to shame in our expectation of Thy mercy, but grant us, O Lord, all our petitions which are unto salvation, and make us worthy to love and fear Thee with all our hearts, and to do Thy will in all things. For Thou art a good God and lovest mankind, and unto Thee we ascribe glory: to the Father, and to the Son, and to the Holy Spirit, now and ever, and unto ages and ages. Amen.

Liturgy of the Presanctified Gifts

The Haven of Thy Will

O Lord, in Thy displeasure rebuke us not, neither chasten us in Thy wrath, but deal with us according to Thy tenderness, O Physician and Healer of our souls. Guide us unto the haven of Thy will. Enlighten the eyes of our hearts unto the knowledge of Thy Truth, and grant unto us that the remainder of the present day and the whole time of our life may be peaceful and sinless, through the intercessions of the Mother of God and of all the saints.

Liturgy of the Presanctified Gifts

I Have Disfigured the Beauty

I persist in caring only for my outer garment, while neglecting the temple within — one made in the image of God.

Through love of pleasure has my form become deformed and the beauty of my inward being been ruined.

A woman will search her house for one lost coin until she finds it. But in me has been lost the beauty of my original image, buried in the passions. Come now, O Savior, search to recover it.

Like the sinful woman I will cry to Thee, O Savior, "I have sinned." I alone have sinned against Thee! Accept my tears as you once did hers when she came to anoint your feet.

Like the Publican I will cry to Thee: "Have pity on me, O Savior." Have pity on me, for among the children of Adam none has sinned more than I!

I have no tears, no change of heart, no remorse — O my God and Savior, grant these to me!

O Lover of mankind, whose wish it is that all be saved, in Thy goodness receive me as I return to Thee.

Give ears to the groaning of my soul, and accept the tears that fall from mine eyes, O Savior, and save me.

Great Canon of St. Andrew of Crete

Arise, O Soul!

My soul, my soul: arise!
Why are you sleeping?
The end is at hand; destruction hangs over you.
Come again to your senses,
That you may be spared by Christ our God,
Who is everywhere present and fills all things.

*

From the depths of Hell
I cried with all my heart to our merciful God,
And he heard me.
And he raised up my life from corruption.

Great Canon of St Andrew of Crete

Deification

There is nothing so sacred as a human being to whom God has imparted of His nature. Consider this . . . Who is it who "will come upon the clouds with power and great glory," [30] shining with incomparable splendor? It will be a human person, though certainly one like God. Each of us will then truly be able to shine more brightly than the sun, to rise on the clouds to see that body of God, to be uplifted to Him and fly towards Him, to approach Him and to be favorably regarded by Him. For when the Master appears the chorus of the good servants will surround Him, and when He shines brightly they too will shine.

What a sight — to see a countless multitude of luminaries above the clouds, an incomparable company of persons exalted as a people of gods surrounding God! The fair ones surrounding the Fair One, the servants surrounding the Master! . . . But Christ . . . regards them as friends. Towards them He observes rules of friendship which He has established from the beginning; He shares His own with them, not merely one or another part of His riches, but He gives the very kingdom, the very crown....What is so full of delight that it could vie with that vision of a chorus of blessed ones, a multitude of those who rejoice? Christ descends from heaven like lightning to earth, while the earth hands back other suns to the Sun of Righteousness, and all is filled with light.

St Nicholas Cabasilas

The Crown of Creation

Know to what extent the Creator has honored you above all the rest of creation. The sky is not an image of God, nor is the moon, nor the sun, nor the beauty of the stars, nor anything of what can be seen in creation. You alone have been made the image of the Reality that transcends all understanding, the likeness of imperishable beauty, the imprint of true divinity, the recipient of beatitude, the seal of the true light. When you turn to him you become that which he is himself....Nothing in creation can be compared with your greatness. God is able to measure the whole heaven with his span. The earth and the sea are enclosed in the hollow of his hand. And although he is so great and holds all creation in the palm of his hand, you are able to hold him, he dwells in you and moves within you without constraint, for he has said, "I will live and move among them."[31]

St Gregory of Nyssa

Flame

We should love the Lord as we do our friends. Many a time I have seen people bring grief to God, without being bothered about it, and I have seen these very same people resort to every device, plan, pressure, plea, and gift, simply to restore an old relationship between friends upset by some minor grievance.

At the beginning of our religious life, we cultivate the virtues, and we do so with toil and difficulty. Progressing a little, we then lose our sense of grief or retain very little of it. But when our mortal intelligence turns to zeal and is mastered by it, then we work with full joy, determination, desire, and a holy flame....

Let all those coming to this marvelous, tough, and painful — though also easy — contest leap, as it were, into a fire, so that a non-material flame may take up residence within them. But let each one test himself, draw food and drink from the bread of pain and the cup of weeping, lest he march himself to judgment.

St John Climacus

What is Prayer

Prayer is by nature a dialog and a union of man with God. Its effect is to hold the world together. It achieves a reconciliation with God. Prayer is the mother and daughter of tears. It is an expiation of sin, a bridge across temptation, a bulwark against affliction. It wipes out conflict, is the work of angels, and is the nourishment of everything spiritual. Prayer is future gladness, action without end, wellspring of virtues, source of grace, hidden progress, food of the soul, enlightenment of mind, an axe against despair, hope demonstrated, sorrow done away with....It is a mirror of progress, a demonstration of success, evidence of one's condition, the future revealed, a sign of glory. For the one who really prays it is the court, the judgment hall, the tribunal of the Lord — and this prior to the judgment that is to come.

St John Climacus

Lament for Paradise Lost

When the enemy tempted me,
I disobeyed Thy command, O Lord.
I exchanged the glory of my immortal body
for shame and nakedness.
Now I must wear garments of skins and fig-leaves;
I am condemned to eat the bread of bitter hardship,
by the sweat of my brow.
The earth is cursed, and brings forth thorns and husks for
me.
O Lord, Thou didst take flesh from the Virgin
in the fullness of time:
Call me back and restore me to Eden!

O Paradise! Garden of delight and beauty,
Dwelling-place made perfect by God,
Unending gladness and eternal joy,
The hope of prophets and the home of the saints:
By the music of thy rustling leaves,
beseech the Creator of all
to open to me the gates which my sins have closed,
That I may partake of the tree of life and grace
Which was given to me in the beginning.

Hymns sung on the eve of the Sunday of Forgiveness

A Prayer to the Mother of God

O my most holy Lady, the Mother of God, by thy holy and all-powerful prayers remove from me, thy humble and burdened servant, despair, forgetfulness, lack of understanding and negligence, and take away all unclean, crafty and blameworthy thoughts from my smitten heart and from my darkened mind; quench the flame of my passions, for I am poor and lost; deliver me from many cruel memories and undertakings, and set me free from all evil actions; for thou art blessed of all generations, and thy most honorable name is glorified unto the ages of ages. Amen.

From the Russian manual of daily prayers.

A Woman's Compunction

The woman had fallen into many sins, O Lord,
Yet when she perceived Thy divinity,
She joined the ranks of the myrrh-bearing women.
In tears she brought Thee myrrh before Thy burial.
She cried, "Woe is me!
For night surrounds me, dark and moonless,
And stings my lustful passion with the love of sin.
But accept the fountain of my tears,
O Thou who didst gather the waters of the sea into
   clouds.
Bow down Thine ear to the sighing of my heart,
O Thou who didst bow the heavens in Thine
      ineffable condescension.
Once Eve heard Thy footstep in paradise
      in the cool of the day,
And in fear she ran and hid herself.
But now I will tenderly embrace those pure feet
      and wipe them with the hair of my head.
Who can measure the multitude of my sins,
Or the depths of Thy judgments, O Savior of my soul?
Do not despise Thy servant in Thine immeasurable
      mercy."

Hymn of Kassia

Seeing the Sky

The eyes are lifted up to look at the sky. The image of the sky is impressed on what is called the retina, and as soon as the image appears there, the message is received in a flash by the express carriers of the nerves to the brain, which is the source of the entire nervous system. And as soon as the contact is made there, the mind is immediately aroused to see the sky. After this perception the mind, by exercising its rational thought, can wonder at the order, the size, the beauty, the light, and all the other attributes of the sky. And in all of these, the contemplative man can see the wisdom, the creativity, the power and the beauty of him who created it. He can thus reason and say: If the sky which is created is so beautiful, so full of light, how much more beautiful and more luminous is the Creator of the sky?...And so the mind climbs as high as it possibly can to the knowledge of the Creator, and with this knowledge the mind excites the heart and the will to love this Creator.

St Basil encouraged us to think such thoughts and through them to rise from the visible to the invisible and from the ephemeral to the eternal. He wrote: "If these ephemeral things are so wonderful, how much more are the eternal? And if the visible are so good, how much more good are the invisible? If the magnitude of heaven goes beyond the ability of human reason to measure, which mind can discern the nature of divine things?"

St Nicodemos of the Holy Mountain

Learning by Example

St Anthony, in turn, subjected himself in all sincerity to
the pious men whom he visited and made it his endeavor
to learn for his own benefit how each was superior to him
in zeal and practice. He observed the graciousness of one,
the earnestness of prayer in another; studied the even
temper of one and the kindheartedness of another; fixed
his attention on the vigils kept by one and on the studies
pursued by another; admired one for his patient endurance
and another for his fasting and sleeping on the ground;
watched closely this man's meekness and the forbearance
shown by another; and in one and all alike he marked
especially devotion to Christ and the love they had for one
another... He thus assimilated in himself what he had
obtained from each and devoted all his energies to realizing in himself the virtues of all.

St Athanasius of Alexandria's Life of Anthony

The Need for Consultation

In the book of Proverbs it says, "Those who have not guidance fall like leaves, but there is safety in much counsel."[32] Take a good look at this saying, brothers. Look at what Scripture is teaching us. It assures us that we should not set ourselves up as guide posts, that we should not consider ourselves sagacious, that we should not believe we can direct ourselves. We need assistance, we need guidance in addition to God's grace.

Concerning those who make a report about what concerns their interior life and do everything with counsel, it says, "There is safety in much counsel." When it says "much counsel" it does not mean taking counsel from all and sundry, but clearly from someone in whom he has full confidence. And he should not be silent about some things and speak about others, but he should report everything and take counsel about everything.

Do not ponder what you should do if you have no one to ask. If anyone really in truth desires the will of God with all his heart, God never leaves him to himself but always guides him according to His will. If a man really sets his heart upon the will of God, God will enlighten a little child to tell that man what is His will.

Dorotheos of Gaza

Mary, the Mother of God

When you are about to pray to the Mother of God, be firmly assured that you will not depart from her without mercy. It is meet and right to think thus, to have this confidence in her. She is the all-merciful Mother of the all-merciful God, and her merciful gifts — incalculably great, innumerable — have been declared from all ages by the Church. To pray to her without such assurance would be foolish and insolent, for such doubt would offend her goodness, just as God's goodness is offended when people pray to Him without hoping to get what they pray for.

When you look upon the icon of the Mother of God, with her Eternal Child, marvel how most truly the Godhead was united with human nature, glorify God's omnipotent goodness, and, recognizing your own dignity as a human person, live worthily of your high calling in Christ — the calling of a child of God, an inheritor of eternal bliss.

Hail, full of grace, the Lord is with thee! So does the holy Church address the all-holy Virgin Mother of God. But the Lord is also with every devout soul that believes in Him; it is not only with her that He abides: *The Lord is with thee* — these words may be addressed to everyone who keeps the Lord's commandments.

St John of Kronstadt

The Communion of Saints

We ought to have the most lively spiritual union with the dwellers in heaven, the apostles, prophets, martyrs, saintly bishops, confessors, with all the saints, as they are all members of the one body, the Church of Christ, to which we sinners also belong, and the living Head of which is the Lord Jesus Christ Himself. This is why we call upon them in prayer, converse with them, thank and praise them. It is urgently necessary for every Christian to be in union with them if he desires to make Christian progress; for the saints are our friends, our guides to salvation, who pray and intercede for us.

As in the earthly life there are poor and rich, so also in the spiritual life, in the spiritual order, there are poor and rich. As the poor ask charity of the rich, and cannot live without help from them, so also in the spiritual order the poor must have recourse to the rich. We are the spiritually poor, while the saints, and those who live in the present life by their faith and piety, are the spiritually rich. It is to them that we needy ones must have recourse. We must beg from their prayers that they may help us to become simple as children, that they may teach us spiritual wisdom, how to conquer sins, how to love God and our neighbor. May the saints of God pray for us, that we may become like unto them.

St John of Kronstadt

The Icon and the Human Person

The icon never strives to stir the emotions of the faithful. Its task is not to provoke in them one or another natural human emotion, but to guide every emotion as well as the reason and all the other faculties of human nature on the way towards transfiguration. Sanctification by grace does not eliminate any faculties of human nature, just as fire does not eliminate the properties of iron. In the same way the icon, in depicting a person's body with all its peculiarities, does not eliminate anything human: it does not exclude either the psychological or the worldly element. It also transmits the feelings of a person...his knowledge, his artistic creativity and the particular external occupation, be it ecclesiastical or temporal, which the given saint has transformed into spiritual endeavor. But, just as in the Holy Scriptures, the whole load of human thoughts, feelings and knowledge is represented in the icon at its point of contact with the world of Divine Grace, and in this contact all that is not purified is burnt up as by fire. Every manifestation of human nature acquires meaning, becomes illumined, finds its true place and significance. Thus it is precisely in the icon that all human feelings, thoughts and actions, as well as the body itself, are given their full value.

Leonid Ouspensky

Icon of the Urban Sky

It is difficult to pray without icons. An icon focuses our prayerful attention, as a magnifying glass focuses diffused sunlight into a spot of intense brightness. The Church Fathers teach that icons proclaim the reality of Christ's humanity. Rejecting icons means renouncing the reality of the Incarnation, i.e., the human nature of Jesus, God and Man.

Yet in our world today, prayer is experienced in strange ways. I was spending the night in a new section of Moscow. Out of the incongruously huge window I could see the cold panorama of endless new modern buildings. There were no icons in the room, but I wanted to pray and stepped to the window. It was better to face that threatening Martian landscape, I thought, than to huddle in a corner pretending that nothing had changed. Suddenly, I felt that I was praying, easily and simply, as if really nothing had happened. I was praying as if the sky were my icon and it was so close. Suddenly I felt that heaven is my home and the spaces round me are not frightening. I felt that man is free in his Christian faith.

Fr Sergei Fudel

The Tree of Life

Greatly saddened was the Tree of Life
when it beheld Adam stolen away from it;
it sank down into the virgin ground and was hidden,
only to burst forth and reappear on Golgotha.
Humanity, like birds that are chased,
took refuge in it
so that it might return them to their proper home.
The chaser was chased away, while the doves
that had been chased
now hop with joy in Paradise.

St Ephrem the Syrian

The Fragrance of Humanity

The humble man approaches wild animals, and the moment they catch sight of him their ferocity is tamed. They come up and cling to him as to their master, wagging their tails and licking his hands and feet. They scent as coming from him the same fragrance that came from Adam before the transgression, the time when they were gathered together before him and he gave them names in Paradise. This scent was taken away from us, but Christ has renewed it and given it back to us at his coming. It is this which has sweetened the fragrance of humanity.

St Isaac the Syrian

Two Abbas, Two Ways

It was told of a brother who came to see Abba Arsenius at Scetis that, when he came to the church, he asked the clergy if he could visit Abba Arsenius...So, because Arsenius' cell was far away, they sent a brother with him. Having knocked on the door, they entered, greeted the old man and sat down without saying anything. Then the brother from the church said, "I will leave you. Pray for me." Now the visiting brother, not feeling at ease with the old man, said "I will come with you," and they went away together. Then the visitor asked, "Take me to Abba Moses, who used to be a robber." When they arrived the Abba welcomed them joyfully and then took leave of them with delight. The brother who had brought the other one said to his companion, "See, I have taken you to the foreigner [Arsenius] and to the Egyptian [Moses], which of the two do you prefer?" "As for me," he replied, "I prefer the Egyptian."

Now a Father who heard this prayed to God saying, "Lord, explain this matter to me: for Thy name's sake, the one flees from men, and the other, for Thy name's sake, receives them with open arms." Then two large boats were shown to him on a river and he saw Abba Arsenius and the Spirit of God sailing in the one, in perfect peace; and in the other was Abba Moses with the angels of God, and they were all eating honey cakes.

Prayers for the Living and the Dead

Blessed art Thou, O Lord, teach me Thy statutes.
The choir of saints have found the fountain of life and the
door of paradise;
May I also find the way through repentance.
I am a lost sheep: call me, O Saviour, and save me.

Blessed art Thou, O Lord, teach me Thy statutes.
I am the image of Thine ineffable glory, though I bear the
brands of transgressions.
Pity Thy creature, O Master, and purify me by Thy
loving kindness.
Grant me the homeland of my heart's desire,
making me again a citizen of paradise.

Blessed art Thou, O Lord, teach me Thy statutes.
Give rest to the soul of Thy servant, O God, and
establish him in Paradise.
Where the choirs of the saints and the just, O Lord,
shine like the stars of heaven.
Give rest to Thy servant who has fallen asleep,
overlooking all his transgressions.

Orthodox Funeral Service

The Birth of God

Do not be amazed, O Mother,
seeing me now as a babe
whom the Father begat from the womb
before the morning star.
For I have come to restore and to glorify with myself the
fallen nature of mortal man,
that magnifies thee in faith and in love.

Today He who holds the whole creation in His hand is
born of a virgin.
He whose essence none can touch is bound in
swaddling clothes as a mortal man.
God, who in the beginning fashioned the heavens, lies in
a manger.
He who rained manna on His people in the
wilderness is fed on milk from His mother's breast.
The Bridegroom of the Church summons the wise men;
The Son of the virgin accepts their gifts.
We worship Thy birth, O Christ.
We worship Thy birth, O Christ.
We worship Thy birth, O Christ.
Show us also Thy Holy Theophany!

Hymns sung on Christmas Eve

The Crucified God

Do not lament me, O Mother,
Seeing me in the tomb,
The Son conceived in the womb without seed
For I shall arise and be glorified with eternal glory as God
I shall exalt all who magnify thee in faith and in love.

Today, He who hung the earth upon the waters
is hung on the tree.
The King of the Angels is decked with a crown of thorns.
He who wraps the heavens in clouds is wrapped
in the purple of mockery.
He who freed Adam in the Jordan is slapped on the face.
The Bridegroom of the Church is affixed to the cross with
nails.
The Son of the virgin is pierced by a spear.
We worship Thy passion, O Christ.
We worship Thy passion, O Christ.
We worship Thy passion, O Christ.
Show us also Thy glorious resurrection!

Hymns sung on Holy Friday

Neighbor

Going to town one day to sell some small articles, Abba Agathon met a cripple on the roadside, paralyzed in his legs, who asked him where he was going. Abba Agathon replied, "To town, to sell some things." The other said, "Do me the favor of carrying me there." So he carried him to the town. The cripple said to him, "Put me down where you sell your wares." He did so. When he had sold an article, the cripple asked, "What did you sell it for?" and he told him the price. The other said, "Buy me a cake," and he bought it. When Abba Agathon had sold a second article, the sick man asked, "How much did you sell it for?" And he told him the price of it. Then the other said "Buy me this," and he bought it. When Agathon, having sold all his wares, wanted to go, he said to him, "Are you going back?" and he replied, "Yes." Then said he, "Do me the favor of carrying me back to the place where you found me." Once more picking him up, he carried him back to that place. Then the cripple said, "Agathon, you are filled with divine blessings, in heaven and on earth." Raising his eyes, Agathon saw no man, it was an angel of the Lord, come to try him.

Anger

Abba Agathon said, "I have never gone to sleep with a grievance against anyone, and, as far as I could, I have never let anyone go to sleep with a grievance against me."

The same abba said, "A man who is angry, even if he were to raise the dead, is not acceptable to God."

Abba Ammonas said, "I have spent fourteen years in Scetis asking God night and day to grant me the victory over anger."

From this Minute

If we love someone, then we always think of that one, we strive to please that one; day and night our heart is preoccupied with that object. Is it in this way that you love God? Do you often turn to Him, do you always remember Him, do you always pray to Him and fulfill His holy commandments? For our good, for our happiness, at least let us give a vow to ourselves, that from this day, from this hour, from this minute we shall strive above all else to love God and to fulfill His holy will!

St Herman of Alaska

Invocation

O Trinity,
beyond being,
beyond divinity,
beyond goodness,
the Christians' guide in the knowledge of divine things:

Lead us in a straight path to the highest summit of the mystical scripture, which is beyond unknowing, and beyond brightness,

where the simple, absolute and unchangeable mysteries of God lie hidden, in the hidden mystery of silent, dazzling darkness.

In the deepest darkness they enlighten with overwhelming brightness that which is beyond manifestation,

they fill our unseen minds with a splendor that is beyond beauty, to plenitude beyond plenitude.

Dionysius the Areopagite

Accomplished and Perfected

The mystery of Thy dispensation, O Christ our God, has
been accomplished and perfected as far as it
was in our power;
For we have kept the memorial of Thy death,
We have seen the figure of Thy resurrection,
We have been filled with Thine unending life,
We have rejoiced in Thine unfailing joy.
Grant that we may all be counted worthy of that same joy
also in the age to come,
Through the grace of Thine eternal Father,
And Thine holy and good and life-creating Spirit,
Now and ever and unto ages of ages.
Amen.

Liturgy of St Basil the Great

Notes, Sources and Biblical References

Notes and sources within the main text are given first and are followed by biblical references.

page

10   1) Acts 17:22–34
      2) Col. 1:17
      3) From Ode 7 and Ikos of the Akathist *Glory to God for All Things*.

11   4) Other languages of the Christian East included Arabic, Syriac, Armenian, Georgian and Coptic.

12   5) "Fathers" and "patristic" are standard terms that are not meant to be exclusive of Christian authors and leaders of the Church who were women. These represent a small but vital minority. Likewise, when the translations in this book use the terms "man" or "men" to speak of the human person in general, they are meant to be understood as inclusive of women.

13   6) Normative texts or events, or more literally, "places where one locates theology."
      7) Numbers in parentheses refer to readings in the main section of the book.

14   8) *The Roots of Christian Mysticism*, (London: New City, 1993), p. 132.

15   9) See George Bebis's introduction to the Paulist Press edition of St Nicodemos of the Holy Mountain (New York, 1989), p. 23.

16   10) Introduction to Benedicta Ward, SLG, trans., *The Sayings of the Desert Fathers*, (Kalamazoo, MI: Cistercian Publications, 1975), pp. viii f.

17   11) Crestwood, NY: SVS Press, 1976, (originally published in Paris, 1944).

20   12) *The Jesus Prayer*, (Crestwood, NY: SVS Press, 1987), p. 13.
      13) Originally published in French as *Sources*, (Paris: Editions Stock, 1982).

21   *The Way of the Ascetics*, (San Francisco: Harper & Row, 1982),
      14) pp. 1-3 (emphasis original). Also publ. Crestwood, NY: SVS Press, 1985. Tito Colliander, born 1904 in St Petersburg, lived most of his life as part of the Swedish-speaking minority of Finland. He was an

artist and creative writer, a married man, who in 1952 wrote this
classic series of exhortations to asceticism.
14) Luke 15:20

22   *Antirrheticus* 41 (GNO III.i, 198) and *Homilies on the Song of Songs,*
     5, (GNO VI, 160-1). St Gregory of Nyssa, youngest of the three Cap-
     padocian Fathers (the other two were Basil the Great and Gregory of
     Nazianzus, "the Theologian"), who flourished in the second half of the
     fourth century.

23   *Homilies on the Song of Songs,* I (PG 44,765; GNO VI, 15f)
     15) I Timothy 2:4
     16) Deuteronomy 6:5

24   G.E.H. Palmer, P. Sherrard, K. Ware, eds., trans., *The Philokalia:
     The Complete Text* (vol iii), (London/Boston: Faber & Faber, 1984), p.
     337. Symeon Metaphrastes, who flourished in the late 10th-early 11th
     centuries, adapted the body of homilies originally attributed to the 4th
     century St Macarius of Egypt. This adaptation was selected for inclu-
     sion by St Nicodemus of the Holy Mountain and St Macarius of
     Corinth in the *Philokalia.*

25   *The Life in Christ,* VI, 6, (Crestwood, NY: SVS Press, 1974)
     pp. 167-8. St Nicholas Cabasilas, 14th century lay theologian, mystical
     writer, commentator on the Church's sacraments and liturgy.
     17) Isaiah 58:9 (LXX)

26   *The Ladder of Divine Ascent,* Step 27, C. Luibheid and N. Russell,
     trans., *John Climacus: The Ladder of Divine Ascent,* (New York: Paulist
     Press, 1982), p. 266. St. John Climacus, 7th century, anchorite for
     40 years, later abbot of Sinai. *The Ladder* is an ascetical work of pro-
     found influence in the Orthodox Church, particularly among monastics.

27   *The Ladder of Divine Ascent,* Step 1, (Paulist Press, p. 74).

28   *Questions and Responses,* Letter 10, (trans. Savas S. Zembillas, unpub
     lished). St Barsanuphius the Great (+542) and his disciple, John the
     Prophet, recluses associated with a monastery near Gaza, conducted a
     joint ministry of spiritual direction by letter. 850 of these letters survive.
     18) Matthew 25:21

29   *Questions and Responses,* Letters 77; 154, (trans. Savas S. Zembillas,
     unpublished).
     19) Psalm 101:5, (LXX)

30   Homily 18, vii f. See G.A. Maloney, trans., *Pseudo-Macarius: The
     Fifty Spiritual Homilies* and the *Great Letter,* (New York: Paulist
     Press, 1992), p. 144 (translation altered). These homilies were attrib-
     uted to the 4th-century Macarius the Great of Egypt. It now appears

more likely that they were written by a Syrian monastic author in the 5th century.

31   Homily 71. (cf. Dana Miller, ed., trans., *The Ascetical Homilies of St Isaac the Syrian,* (Boston: Holy Transfiguration Monastery, 1984) pp. 344f., also in *Daily Readings with St Isaac of Syria,* (Springfield, IL: Templegate) p. 29). St Isaac of Syria, 7th century monastic, briefly bishop of Nineveh. A "doctor of the soul." Wrote in Syriac, a language close to Aramaic.

32   *Great Catechetical Oration,* 24 (Trans. E.R. Hardy, in *The Christology of the Later Fathers,* (Philadelphia: Westminster Press, 1954), pp. 300f.).

33   *Humanistic and Theanthropic Education,* in Asterios Gerostergios, trans., *Orthodox Faith and Life in Christ,* (115 Gilbert Road, Belmont, MA: Institute for Byzantine and Modern Greek Studies, 1994) p. 55. Fr Justin Popovich (+1979), monastic father, teacher and intellectual, with a large and devoted following, particularly in his native Serbia. 20) Matthew 5:48

34   St Basil the Great, eldest of the Cappadocian Fathers, brother of Gregory of Nyssa and Macrina the Younger, is author of one of the Orthodox Church's chief liturgies. (The petition for travelers 'by air' was brought into use in the 20th Century.)

35   From the Apostikha of Matins, Tuesday in Holy Week.

36   *My Life in Christ* (cf. W.J. Grisbrooke, ed., *Spiritual Counsels. Select Passages from* My Life in Christ, (Crestwood, NY: SVS Press 1967), pp. 76,78). St John of Kronstadt (1829-1908), married Russian priest, renowned for his spiritual guidance, and also for the way in which he celebrated the divine liturgy. A "bearer of Christian joy." 21) Mt. 10:19-20

37   *Light in the Darkness,* trans. Sophie Koulomzin, (Crestwood, NY: SVS Press, 1989), p. 26. Fr Sergei Fudel (1901-1977), married Russian priest, bearer of light and love for the Church during and beyond his years in prison and exile at the hands of the Communist régime.

38   *On the Treachery of Judas,* I, vi (PG 49, 381), and *On Matthew* 50, iii (PG 58,508). St John Chrysostom (c. 347-407), one of the great orators of the Church (his name means "golden-mouthed"), preached dynamic and practical sermons drawing particularly from the gospels and St Paul's writings.

39   Sergei Hackel, *Pearl of Great Price,* (Crestwood, NY: SVS Press, 1982), pp. 29f. Mother Maria Skobtsova (1891-1945), Russian émigré intellectual in Paris where, as a monastic, she founded shelters and

kitchens for the poor. She died in a concentration camp.
22) cf. Matthew 25:35-43

40   *Fourth Century on Love,* 63-66. See G.E.H. Palmer, P. Sherrard, K.
      Ware, eds., trans., *The Philokalia: The Complete Text* (vol ii), (Lon-
      don/Boston: Faber & Faber, 1981), p. 108 (translation altered). St
      Maximus the Confessor (580-662), ascetical writer and theologian.
      23) I Timothy 4:8
      24) Galatians 5:16

41   *Concerning Continual Communion,* cf. C. Cavarnos, *St. Macarius of
      Corinth,* (115 Gilbert Road, Belmont, MA: Institute for Byzantine and
      Modern Greek Studies, 1972) pp. 78-80. Macarius of Corinth (1731-
      1805), at the center of the moral and spiritual revival of 18th-century
      Greece, writer, bishop and, together with Nicodemos of the Holy
      Mountain, compiler of the *Philokalia.*
      25) John 6:55

42   Benedicta Ward, SLG, trans., *The Sayings of the Desert Fathers,*
      (Kalamazoo, MI: Cistercian Publications, 1975), pp. 71: 193. Mothers
      Theodora and Syncletica (4th century Alexandria) are two of the few
      women who appear in the alphabetical collection of Apophthegmata, or
      Sayings of the Desert Fathers.

43   Benedicta Ward, SLG, trans., *The Sayings of the Desert Fathers,* p. 2.

44   *The Communion of Love,* (Crestwood, NY: SVS Press, 1984), pp. 34-
      5. Matta El-Meskin, erstwhile hermit, now spiritual father of the Monas-
      tery of St Macarius in the Egyptian desert. He is of the ancient Coptic
      Church, with which, it is hoped, the Eastern Orthodox Church will
      soon again be in communion.
      26) Rev. 3:20

45   cf. *The Life of Anthony and The Letter to Marcellinus,* (New York:
      Paulist, 1980), p. 75. St Anthony the Great (+356) is considered
      the father of desert monasticism, through whose life and work "the
      desert became a city of monks." His biography is ascribed to St
      Athanasius (+373).

46   *On the Will of God, and on Freedom,* in Archimandrite Sophrony
      (Sakharov), *Saint Silouan the Athonite,* trans. Rosemary Edmonds,
      (Tolleshunt Knights, Essex, U.K.: Stavropegic Monastery of St John
      the Baptist, 1991) pp. 335f. St Silouan (1866-1938), monk at the
      Russian monastery of St Panteleimon on Mount Athos.

47   *We Shall See Him as He Is,* trans. Rosemary Edmonds, (Tolleshunt
      Knights, Essex, U.K.: Stavropegic Monastery of St John the Baptist,
      1988) pp. 119f. Archimandrite Sophrony (1896-1993), Athonite monk

and spiritual father, disciple of St Silouan, founder of the Monastery of St John the Baptist in Essex, England.

27) cf. Revelation 3:20

48   Conversation with Motovilov (cf. G.P. Fedotov, ed., *A Treasury of Russian Spirituality*, (London: Sheed and Ward, 1950), pp. 266, 268). St Seraphim of Sarov (1759-1833), forest hermit, then spiritual father to countless monastics and lay people. He would greet his visitors with the words "Christ is Risen, my joy!" Together with St Sergius of Radonezh, one of Russia's greatest and most beloved saints.

49   The first is a prayer to the Holy Spirit which is traditionally recited at the start of liturgical and private prayer. The second is excerpted from the Hymn of Degrees, sung at Matins.

50   *The Power of the Name*, (Fairacres, Oxford: SLG Press, 1974). Bishop Kallistos (Ware), author of several books and articles, translator of the *Philokalia* and of liturgical texts, university teacher (at Oxford), and pastor.

28) Galatians 2:20

29) John 3:30

51   These prayers, from the Russian Orthodox Prayer Book, are usually ascribed to Philaret of Moscow (+1867). The first is also related to a prayer ascribed to Hieromonk Parthenius of the Kiev Caves Monastery.

52   This prayer is recited at the close of each reading of the office of the Hours during the course of the day.

53   This prayer, recited many times daily during Lent at church services and privately, is traditionally attributed to St Ephrem of Syria (306-373), most of whose voluminous writing is in verse.

54   *The Power of the Name.*

55   *The Sacrament of Love*, (Crestwood, NY: SVS Press, 1985), pp. 61-3. Paul Evdokimov (1901-1970), Russian émigré lay theologian, taught at St Sergius Institute in Paris. This book, together with its companion *Woman and the Salvation of the World*, explores vital themes that were for the most part only latent in patristic writing.

56   Prayer of the third Antiphon.

57   Prayer of the second Antiphon.

58   *Great Canon*, Canticle II. St Andrew of Crete (+740), certainly best known for this masterpiece, which poetically expounds on its penitential theme, constantly weaving in scriptural texts. Mournful yet full of hope and the praise of God, it is appropriate that it is sung during the first week of the Great Fast.

59   Oikos and Kontakion from Canticle VI.

60   *The Life in Christ* VI, 5 (SVS pp. 166f.).
     30) Matthew 24:30
61   *Homilies on the Song of Songs*, II (PG 44, 805f; GNO VI, 68). In O.
     Clément, *The Roots of Christian Mysticism*, (London, New City, 1993),
     p. 79.
     31) 2 Corinthians 6:16
62   *The Ladder of Divine Ascent*, Step I (cf. Paulist ed., pp. 77;76).
63   *The Ladder of Divine Ascent*, Step 28 (Paulist ed., p. 274).
64   The day before the beginning of Great Lent marks the remembrance of
     the expulsion of Adam and Eve from Paradise. It is also the Sunday of
     Forgiveness.
66   This hymn, composed by the ninth-century monastic poetess Kassia (or
     Kassiani), is sung at Matins on Holy Wednesday. On this day the
     Orthodox commemorate the woman who came to anoint Jesus before
     his crucifixion (cf. Luke 7:36-50).
67   *A Handbook of Spiritual Counsel I*, (trans. P.A. Chamberas, (New
     York: Paulist Press, 1989) p. 71). St Nicodemos of the Holy Mountain
     (1749-1809), voluminous writer, compiler/editor of several of the
     Church's major ascetical texts including the *Philokalia*, the *Ever-
     getinos*, a collection of the letters of Sts Barsanuphius and John, and
     Unseen Warfare (adapted from a 16th-century Italian work).
68   *The Life of St. Anthony*. This translation is by Robert T. Meyer,
     (Westminster, MD: Newman Press, 1978).
69   "On the Need for Consultation", *Discourses and Sayings*, (Kalama-
     zoo, MI: Cistercian Publications, 1977), pp. 122f.; 129.
     32) cf. Proverbs 11:14
70   *My Life in Christ* (cf. W.J. Grisbrooke, ed., pp. 62f., translation
     altered).
71   *My Life in Christ* (cf. W.J. Grisbrooke, ed., pp. 64f.).
72   L. Ouspensky and V. Lossky, *The Meaning of Icons*, (Crestwood,
     NY: SVS Press, 1982) p. 39. (Originally published in 1952.) Leonid
     Ouspensky (1905-1987), Russian émigré in Paris, one of the great
     iconographers and iconologists of our age.
73   *Light in the Darkness*, p. 17.
74   *Hymn on Virginity*, XVI.10, trans. Sebastian Brock: cf. the intro-
     duction to his edition of St Ephrem the Syrian's *Hymns on Paradise*,
     (Crestwood, NY: SVS Press, 1990) pp. 60f..
75   Homily 77 (cf. Dana Miller, ed., p. 383, also in *Daily Readings with
     St Isaac of Syria*, p. 69).
76   Benedicta Ward, trans., *The Sayings of the Desert Fathers*, p. 15.

77   Many of the prayers of the Orthodox Funeral service are, like these, geared at least as much towards the living as towards the dead.

79   The parallel with the Christmas hymns is obvious. Here, as there, the emphasis is upon the continuity of person — the Son of God, born before all time of the Father without a mother, the same born for our sake in time of a mother without a father. Orthodox Church hymnography never fails to sing about this paradox.

80   Benedicta Ward, trans., *The Sayings of the Desert Fathers*,p. 22.

81   *Ibid.*, pp. 17f., 20, 22.

82   cf. *Little Russian Philokalia,* Vol. III, *St. Herman of Alaska,* (Platina, CA: St. Herman Press, 1989), pp. 31f. St Herman of Alaska (+1836), Russian hermit missionary to Alaska, celebrated as "North Star of Christ's holy Church."

83   *Mystical Theology I* (PG 3, 997A). The author is probably a fifth or sixth-century writer who assumed the name of Dionysius the Areopagite, the convert of Apostle Paul of whom we read in Acts 17:34. His influence upon Christian theology and spirituality has been immense.

84   This prayer is said by the priest at the close of the Liturgy of St Basil. For a variant translation, cf. C.A. Swainson, ed., *The Greek Liturgies,* (1884), p. 171.

Mother of God.
In Greek: Meter Theou, here shortened to Mer Thu.

The strokes above this monogram denote holiness, as in the conventional symbol of the halo.